Ragdoll Cats

Connie Colwell Miller
AR B.L.: 1.6
Points: 0.5   LG

Pebble®

Ragdoll Cats

by Connie Colwell Miller

Consulting Editor: Gail Saunders-Smith, PhD

Consultant: Jennifer Zablotny, DVM
Member, American Veterinary Medical Association

Capstone
press®
Mankato, Minnesota

Pebble Books are published by Capstone Press,
151 Good Counsel Drive, P.O. Box 669, Mankato, Minnesota 56002.
www.capstonepress.com

1 2 3 4 5 6 13 12 11 10 09 08

Library of Congress Cataloging-in-Publication Data
Miller, Connie Colwell, 1976–
    Ragdoll cats / by Connie Colwell Miller.
    p. cm. — (Pebble books. Cats)
    Includes bibliographical references and index.
    Summary: "Simple text and photographs present an introduction to the
Ragdoll breed, its growth from kitten to adult, and pet care information" — Provided
by publisher.
    ISBN-13: 978-1-4296-1716-1 (hardcover)
    ISBN-10: 1-4296-1716-0 (hardcover)
    1. Ragdoll cat — Juvenile literature. I. Title. II. Series.
SF449.R34M55 2009
636.8'3 — dc22   2007051274

Note to Parents and Teachers

The Cats set supports national science standards related to life
science. This book describes and illustrates Ragdoll cats. The images
support early readers in understanding the text. The repetition of
words and phrases helps early readers learn new words. This book
also introduces early readers to subject-specific vocabulary words,
which are defined in the Glossary section. Early readers may need
assistance to read some words and to use the Table of Contents,
Glossary, Read More, Internet Sites, and Index sections of the book.

Table of Contents

Fluffy Cats

Ragdoll cats have
fluffy coats.
They have long fur
called a ruff
around their necks.

Some Ragdolls have
dark colors
on their points.
Points are a cat's
ears, face, legs, and tail.

Some Ragdolls
have white fur
between their eyes.
Mitted Ragdolls have
white feet.

From Kitten to Adult

Ragdoll kittens are born with blue eyes. Their eyes stay blue when they grow up.

Ragdoll kittens
learn quickly.
Some Ragdolls
learn to play fetch.

Ragdolls grow up
to be large cats.
They can weigh up to
20 pounds (9 kilograms).

Caring for Ragdolls

Ragdolls' long coats may get tangled. They need to be brushed twice each week.

Ragdolls need
food and water
every day.

Ragdolls are
fluffy and sweet.
These loving cats
make great pets.

Glossary

coat — an animal's hair or fur

fetch — to go after something and bring it back

points — the darker areas of fur on a cat's tail, paws, face, and ears

ruff — a ring of long fur around an animal's neck

tangle — to twist together

Read More

Barnes, Julia. *Pet Cats.* Pet Pals. Milwaukee: Gareth Stevens, 2007.

Shores, Erika L. *Caring for Your Cat.* Postively Pets. Mankato, Minn.: Capstone Press, 2007.

Internet Sites

FactHound offers a safe, fun way to find Internet sites related to this book. All of the sites on FactHound have been researched by our staff.

Here's how:

1. Visit *www.facthound.com*

2. Choose your grade level.

3. Type in this book ID **1429617160** for age-appropriate sites. You may also browse subjects by clicking on letters, or by clicking on pictures and words.

4. Click on the **Fetch It** button.

FactHound will fetch the best sites for you!

Index

Word Count: 118
Grade: 1
Early-Intervention Level: 12

Editorial Credits
Lori Shores, editor; Renée T. Doyle, set designer; Danielle Ceminsky, book designer; Wanda Winch, photo researcher

Photo Credits
iStockphoto/Bonita Hein, 4
Kimball Stock/Alan Robinson, 6
Peter Arnold/Biosphoto/Klein J.-L. & Hubert M.-L., 14
Shutterstock/Dave Wetzel, 1, 22, cover; Simone van den Berg, 10
Ulrike Schanz Photodesign & Animal Stock, 8, 12, 16, 18, 20